SCHOPENHAUER IN 90 MINUTES

Schopenhauer
IN 90 MINUTES

Paul Strathern

IVAN R. DEE
CHICAGO

SCHOPENHAUER IN 90 MINUTES. Copyright © 1999 by
Paul Strathern. All rights reserved, including the right to
reproduce this book or portions thereof in any form. For
information, address: Ivan R. Dee, Publisher, 1332 North
Halsted Street, Chicago 60622. Manufactured in the United
States of America and printed on acid-free paper.

Library of Congress Cataloging-in-Publication Data:
Strathern, Paul, 1940–
    Schopenhauer in 90 minutes / Paul Strathern
       p. cm. — (Philosophers in 90 minutes)
    Includes bibliographical references and index.
    ISBN 1-56663-263-3 (cloth : alk. paper). —
ISBN 1-56663-264-1 (paper : alk. paper)
    1. Schopenhauer, Arthur, 1788–1860. I. Title. II. Series.
B3148.S78 1999
193—dc21   99-34150

Contents

SCHOPENHAUER IN 90 MINUTES

Introduction

The modern age of philosophy began with Descartes, who doubted everything and reduced our knowledge to one central certainty: "Cogito ergo sum" (I think, therefore I am). Unfortunately he then proceeded to rebuild our knowledge, much as if nothing had happened. After this, the British empiricists Locke, Berkeley, and Hume embarked upon a similarly rigorous destructive process, claiming that our knowledge can only be based on experience. By the time Hume completed this process, human knowledge had been reduced to ruins. According to him, all we in fact experienced was a gibberish of sensations: our conclusions from these had no philosophical validity whatsoever.

This was the absurdity that famously awoke Kant from his "dogmatic slumbers." Taking account of empiricism but refusing to be cowed by it, Kant constructed the greatest of all philosophical systems.

Passing from the sublime to the ridiculous, Hegel then produced his own gross system. His contemporary, Schopenhauer, was to treat this monstrosity with the contempt it deserved. Schopenhauer was to maintain a recognizably Kantian point of view with regard to epistemology (how we know the world). Kant, however, also created a moral system of surpassing beauty and elevation. For Kant, the world had a moral foundation. "Es ist gut" (It is good) were said to be his last words. And in his last great work, which dealt with the purpose of the world, he concluded: "Two things fill the mind with ever new and increasing wonder and awe, the oftener and more steadily we reflect upon them: the starry heavens above me and the moral law within me." As we shall see, Schopenhauer saw it all very differently.

Schopenhauer's Life and Works

With Schopenhauer we return to planet Earth—with a vengeance. As a man, Schopenhauer was a nasty piece of work, but his writings are immensely endearing. Of the great philosophers he was the finest stylist since Plato. His philosophy too is very appealing. It is the first since Socrates to be imbued with the entire personality of the man who propounds it. From Schopenhauer's writings you gain a very clear picture of what he was like as a person—with one proviso that is worth remembering at all times when reading him: what appears as witty, insightful, and destructive of humbug on the page may often be sarcastic, egotistical, and aggressive when encountered in real life. Offstage, comedians are seldom renowned for their human qualities— and just because witty philosophers are so rare doesn't make them an exception to this rule. (Socrates is extremely fortunate that we have no testimony from his wife, Xanthippe.)

But Schopenhauer was original in another, more fundamental way. Not for nothing is he known as the "philosopher of pessimism." With most other major philosophers you can't escape feeling that the writer is on his best behavior, and you're expected to be so too. Everything is all very serious and moral. (Even Hume takes philosophy seriously while doing his demolition job.) Schopenhauer, on the other hand, makes it very plain that he regards the world and our life in it as a bad joke. In this he is undeniably closer to describing the actual state of affairs than those who view the world from an optimistic or pur- posive standpoint. This pessimism was im- mensely refreshing in its day, after centuries of Christianity and latter-day rationalism. But Schopenhauer was a pessimist only in so far as he claimed that the world is indifferent to our fate—it doesn't thwart us *on purpose*.

This was an attitude that had not received full expression since the Stoics, who advocated a mealymouthed withdrawal from the evils of the horrible world. Schopenhauer advocated the same, but he did so in a distinctly combative and worldly manner. And he was far too egotistical to achieve such self-denial in his own life (though in his view he endured an existence of exemplary asceticism). These paradoxes account for much of Schopenhauer's popularity. They stem from a contradiction that lay deep in his character and remained unresolved throughout his life.

Arthur Schopenhauer was born on February 22, 1788, in the Baltic city of Danzig (now the Polish city of Gdansk), just across the gulf from where his lifelong hero Immanuel Kant was living in Königsberg. Schopenhauer's father was a merchant from a patrician family, and his mother was a lively woman with an unfulfilled artistic nature. The family was cosmopolitan in outlook—Arthur was given his name because it was also the same in French and English. When the Prussians, who did not share this zenophile outlook, marched into Danzig in 1793, Schopenhauer's father immediately removed his home and business to the free port of Hamburg. Here the Schopenhauers eventually took up residence in a fine old house in the Altstadt (Old City).

The Schopenhauers' new home was sufficiently grand to contain a paneled ballroom with a stuccoed ceiling, and in the customary manner it backed onto the large warehouses containing the family business which overlooked the Fleet (canal) for unloading barges. The house was one of many where the wealthy merchants of the city lived and entertained each other in stolid bourgeois fashion. It was not homely in any way, and young Arthur grew up a sophisticated little prig receiving (and eventually requiring) little love.

At the age of ten he was sent away for two years to France to learn French, staying with the family of a business friend of his father's in Le Havre. Here he became like a brother to the son of the house, Anthime. When he was fifteen Arthur's parents took him on a two-year grand tour of Europe. In London he was dazzled by Piccadilly and the theatres, but he was then forced to spend several months in "Egyptian darkness" learning English at a school in Wimbledon while his parents toured Scotland. This English private-school education helped make up for all he had missed by not going to a Prussian school—being chased into the pool before breakfast, regular floggings from the masters, English "cuisine," and endless church services. It also helped prepare him for the tourist sights to follow. These included a two-month stay in Bordeaux, in the very house that Hölderlin had fled in a fit of insanity two years earlier, and a visit to Toulon, where *six thousand* galley slaves were chained up in "the dirtiest, most revolting sojourn imaginable." (Years later Schopenhauer was to draw on this horrific image to describe the misery of humanity fettered to the evil of the will to live.) In Bohemia Schopenhauer climbed Mount Schneekoppe, where his reaction has since been found in the chalet visitors' book:

"Who can climb
And remain silent?

Arthur Schopenhauer from Hamburg."

But on the whole this was an immensely depressing time for young Arthur. Wherever the family traveled in Europe, evidence of the misery caused by the recent Napoleonic Wars was all too plain to see. Maimed beggars lined the streets of the cities, many villages were semiderelict, and still Napoleon's megalomania remained unsatisfied. The age that had begun with such hopes at the French Revolution had degenerated into a despair felt all over Europe. This was the period that produced the sophisticated insouciance of Byron, the melancholy lyrics of the great Italian poet Leopardi, "a thoroughly finished world" in the words of Goethe, where Beethoven tore the dedication to Napoleon from his Eroica (Heroic) Symphony.

Schopenhauer was deeply aware of such things and wished to play his own part in the world of culture. But this was not to be. His father browbeat him into becoming a businessman. At the end of his grand tour of Europe, Schopenhauer was forced to abandon his education and become apprenticed to a local business in Hamburg. This was a time of deep—and deeply repressed—personal distress for Schopenhauer. (At the same age, a very similar conflict caused the equally tough-minded Hume to suffer a nervous breakdown.)

Then suddenly Schopenhauer's entire situation changed. In the early hours of April 20, 1805, Schopenhauer's father climbed to the top of the warehouse at the back of the family mansion and flung himself into the Fleet. The precise nexus of reasons for his suicide remains uncertain. His marriage had become something of a painful charade; the European scene was immensely depressing; and business prospects didn't look good. Yet perhaps more pertinent was his deep streak of melancholy (which his son was to inherit) and a family history of mental instability (Arthur's paternal grandmother went insane). But Schopenhauer's mind does not appear to have been affected by madness—there was to be no saner philosopher than Schopenhauer.

The suicide was hushed up, as such unusually profound decisions in high society often are (presumably in case they prove inspirational). The

Schopenhauer business was wound up, leaving the family with a comfortable private income for life; and Arthur's mother and his younger sister left Hamburg to live a new artistic existence in cultural Weimar. Meanwhile the eighteen-year-old Schopenhauer was left alone in the city, working at a job he didn't like but felt obliged to continue with. Shortly before his death, Schopenhauer's father had given him an essay by the poet Matthias Claudius called *To My Son*. This preached a stoic, alienated inwardness which was in deep accord with Schopenhauer's feelings. But he didn't spend his whole time in introspection. As was the case in his later years, Schopenhauer's worldly sophistication allowed him to live a life apparently at deep variance with his innermost feelings. It was during this period that Schopenhauer's friend Anthime, from Le Havre, arrived to study business in Hamburg. They both had money, and on the weekends the two of them went around the stage doors picking up actresses and chorus girls. If they didn't score with them, they would make up for it with "the embraces of an industrious whore."

18

In 1807 Schopenhauer finally summoned up the nerve to disobey his father's wishes. He left Hamburg and went to school in Gotha in order to gain sufficient qualifications to enter university. But by now Schopenhauer was far too mature for school, and he was soon expelled (for writing a not particularly funny or even scurrilous poem about a wet schoolmaster). He then went to live with his mother at Weimar.

Mom had blossomed into a star of the literary salons. She'd started writing and had become friends with the unconventional Grand Old Man of German Literature, Goethe, and the witty Christoph Wieland (the German Voltaire). Madame Schopenhauer was much in demand but had the social daring to scorn proposals of marriage, preferring her independence. Schopenhauer was appalled at the sight of his mother enjoying herself in such a fashion; and she herself didn't fancy having a disapproving son living under the same roof to cramp her style. Both were strong-willed and volatile, and soon fell out. There were several scenes, and much slamming of doors. No doubt Schopenhauer was genuinely shocked by his mother's behavior. (The concept of chauvinist hypocrisy, like Antarctica, had yet to be discovered, though some intrepid explorers of the oceanic emptiness of social life were becoming convinced that it existed.) No doubt Schopenhauer was also jealous of his mother's success in such exalted literary company. He despised his mother's aspirations to "genius" (while harboring similar aspirations himself), and his mother's transformation almost certainly brought to the surface a latent oedipal frisson between them.

Everyone heaved a sigh of relief when young Arthur left in 1809 to study at the University of Göttingen. He enrolled as a medical student but soon began attending lectures in philosophy. It was here that Schopenhauer discovered Plato and then began reading Kant, who was to have such an overwhelming influence on his philosophy. Schopenhauer recognized the superlative skill of Kant's philosophy and found himself bitterly disappointed when he tried studying the more modern work of Hegel. He soon began spreading his intellectual wings in his private notebooks, which reveal his remarkable philosophic acumen rapidly increasing in inverse proportion to his modesty. Schopenhauer came to the opinion that he was a giant among midgets on the philosophical scene in Göttingen; in 1811 he switched to Berlin to study under Fichte, the leading German philosopher of the period. (Hegel had published *The Phenomenology of Mind* four years earlier, but no one had yet pretended that they understood it.) But Schopenhauer quickly became disillusioned with Fichte's obscurantism. What Schopenhauer was looking for was something as clear as science, and equally as convincing.

Despite all this, Schopenhauer was almost persuaded by Fichte's enthusiasm for the War of Liberation to join the German fight against Napoleon. But in the end he thought better of it, and in 1812 he went off to write his doctoral dissertation. This was entitled *On the Fourfold Root of the Principle of Sufficient Reason* and is as interesting as it sounds, being largely a Kantian exploration of the four types of cause and effect (logical, physical, mathematical, and moral).

Schopenhauer now returned to Weimar, where Johanna Schopenhauer had taken up with a court official named Müller (who preferred to be known by the more aristocratic name of von Gerstenbergk). This unfortunate bergk was twelve years Johanna's junior and liked to write poetry. Schopenhauer arrived on the scene and played his Hamlet role to the full. Müller wasn't quite up to playing Claudius and would rise from the dinner table in a fit of pique at Arthur's oblique cutting remarks—leaving the tyro Hamlet to have it out with Gertrude-Johanna. One of Johanna's letters to her son catches the tone. "Not Müller, but you yourself have torn yourself away from me; your mistrust, your criticism of my life, of my choice of friends, your desultory behavior towards me, your contempt for my sex, your greed, your moods. . . ." Johanna was already becoming the figure who would produce the popular romantic novels that made her famous, and her son couldn't bear it. He knew that he had an intellect far superior to hers (which wasn't quite as negligible as many commentators would have us believe). Yet he was not capable

22

of simply dismissing her literary pretensions from his mind as beneath his consideration. This conflict evidently had to run its course in order for unfinished psychological business to be played out.

But Weimar was more than just a soap opera of endless domestic tantrums for Schopenhauer. He also came to know Goethe. The budding philosopher and the mature genius would talk for hours. Schopenhauer later claimed that he "profited immensely" from these conversations, and also that he helped Goethe with his "Theory of Colors." This comes as a surprise, for Schopenhauer had studied medicine and possessed a good scientific brain. Goethe's theory of colors was little more than a hobby of genius—the foible of an amateur scientist, with which he would pester his admiring visitors. A century before, Newton had already explained how white light is composed of all the colors of the spectrum. Goethe obstinately refused to believe what was obvious to anyone who had seen white light pass through a prism, whose refractive power broke it down into the colors of the rainbow. In

23

Goethe's view, white light was a color in its own right. His theory claimed that all colors were in fact a mixture of light and darkness, permeated by a cloudy element that gave the ensuing grey dusk its colored radiance.

This nonsense was taken seriously only because of Goethe's genius in other fields, and then only by the literati and other scientific numskulls. Schopenhauer had considerable literary skill but certainly didn't fall into the latter category. One wonders why he was taken in. For once his arrogance seems to have failed him. This was perhaps the last time Schopenhauer allowed his ideas to be influenced by a living being whose genius he was willing to recognize. From now on he would have sufficient self-certainty to follow his own intuition at all times—often in the teeth of prevailing contemporary opinion. Fortunately Schopenhauer had an exceptional intellectual instinct, which enabled him to produce a philosophy that was not only original but also uncannily prescient of intellectual developments to come— rather than the philosophical equivalent of Goethe's theory of colors, which is the usual product of a thinker who dismisses the ideas of his contemporaries with the derision he feels they deserve.

The young Schopenhauer's admiration for the aging Goethe was deep and heartfelt. And though their friendship was brief, it was the only such warm relationship he was to have in his life. It is no accident that Goethe was almost exactly the same age as Schopenhauer's father would have been had he not committed suicide. Goethe's benevolent brilliance was perhaps the only foil for the austere, powerful shadow of Schopenhauer's dead father. But all this did little to improve things with mother. Goethe hardly helped matters at home when he informed Johanna Schopenhauer that her son would one day be recognized as a genius. In her view there was room for only one of this species on the family perch, and that place was already occupied.

It was also during this period that Schopenhauer discovered Indian philosophy, which together with Plato and Kant were to be the formative influences on his own thinking. Indian philosophy provided an intellectual justification for his deeply pessimistic view of the world. In fact, this justification was as dubious as its source. Schopenhauer read a book called *Oupnekhat*—the latest fad among the romantics, who were willing to take up anything that set their minds free from the constraints of rationalism. The book was a translation by a Frenchman into Latin, from a Persian translation from the original Sanskrit. Its fidelity to the original text is perhaps best illustrated by the closeness of its title, *Oupnekhat,* to what we now call the original: *The Upanishads.* It is ironic that Schopenhauer's questionable use of this questionable text was to provide a solid foundation for modern philosophic pessimism, a strain of thought that remains firmly with us to this day.

In the end the *sturm und drang* (everyday romanticism) in the Schopenhauer household came to a peak, and Arthur slammed his last door. In May 1814 he left Weimar forever. He was never to see his mother again, though she continued to correspond with him sporadically during her coming period of literary stardom. ("You are unbearable and burdensome . . . ," etc.)

For the next few years Schopenhauer lived in Dresden. Here he wrote the thousand-page *The World as Will and Representation,* his greatest work. He saw this work as his solution to the "riddle of the world." Since the very beginning of philosophy, such an aim would have been viewed as laudable—an incontrovertible foundation on which to build one's philosophy. But it's worth noting that Schopenhauer's starting point is by no means necessary (in the logical sense). That is, it is not inevitable. How come? Well, what precisely is this "riddle"? If one confronts the world as a riddle, viewing it as an enigma, a puzzle to be solved, a mystery to be uncovered, and so forth, then there must be an answer. A question (or riddle) implies an answer. But there is in fact no logical reason why we should seek to question the world in Schopenhauer's way. There are many other attitudes we might adopt: rage, acceptance, despair, and so forth. Plato, who was a major influence on Schopenhauer, famously claimed that "philosophy begins in wonder." This "wonder" is open to two interpretations: wonder as awe, and wonder as "why?" Plato seems to have intended the former, but philosophy before and since has emphasized the latter. Not until the twentieth century was this attitude questioned—when philosophy came to regard itself as an activity rather than a search for the "truth." Schopenhauer certainly viewed his philosophy as the latter, or at least as a significant step along the true path to the latter. As he put it: this philosophy "will in future be perfected, worked out more accurately and finely, made more readily comprehensible and easier—but it will never be overthrown. Philosophy will exist; the history of philosophy will be concluded." Philosophers will eventually arrive at the truth, and the riddle will be solved.

Ironically it was Schopenhauer who was to a considerable extent responsible for the undermining of this point of view. His wholly original way of viewing the world was the first step along the path in the *other* direction (though he was unaware that he was taking this momentous step). Instead of viewing the world with awe, Schopenhauer viewed it with disgust. Medieval philosophers had often viewed the world as a

pretty base affair: a theatre of folly and evil, n
less. But there always remained an element of redeeming grace. The world itself may have been
base, but the overall scheme of things was
presided over by a God who was good. When
Schopenhauer saw the world as evil, he meant
that the entire scheme of things was evil, utterly
devoid of any redeeming feature.

In choosing to regard the world as evil rather
than good, Schopenhauer had inadvertently un-
dermined the necessity of his own position. Later
philosophers (especially Nietzsche and Wittgenstein) would realize this. Schopenhauer's attitude
toward the world was contingent (that is, not
logically necessary). Philosophy could adopt any
number of attitudes toward the world. Viewing
it as a riddle was only one of many possible responses—and all were contingent.

Schopenhauer's *The World as Will and Representation* is prefaced, curiously, with a quota-
tion from Rousseau: "Sors l'enfance, ami
réveilletoi!" (in effect: "Grow up and come to
your senses, my friend"). The fundamental idea
of this mammoth book is deftly summed up in its

...cimes misleadingly translated _as Will and Idea_). The world we ...sts of representation, mere phenom- –very much as Kant described it. But what supports this representation is not the ultimate reality of noumena (the thing-in-itself), as in Kant. Instead the entire phenomenal façade of the world, the phenomena we experience, is supported by the universal Will. This Will is blind, permeates all things, and is eternally without purpose. Like Kant's noumena, it is beyond space and time, and has no cause. It is this Will that brings about all the misery and suffering of the world, which can only end in death. Our only hope is to liberate ourselves from the power of this Will and the trappings of individuality and egoism that are at its mercy. This can only be done by selflessness expressed in compassion for our fellow sufferers, by abnegation of the Will as practiced by saints and ascetics of all races and creeds, and by aesthetic appreciation of works of art (which involves will-less contemplation).

In his earliest mature work, _The Fourfold_

Root of the Principle of Sufficient Reason, Schopenhauer had argued that our perception creates the world according to the four types of cause and effect. These are logical, physical, mathematical, and moral, and all conform to the principle of sufficient reason. Schopenhauer adopted the principle of sufficient reason wholesale from its eighteenth-century rationalist originator Gottfried Leibniz, the first of the great German philosophers. Leibniz defined his principle: "Every fact which is true or existent, and any principle which is true, is dependent upon a *sufficient reason* for its being so and not otherwise, even though most of the time we cannot know these reasons." In other words, everything has a reason for its existence—for existing as it is and not otherwise.

Schopenhauer may have taken over this principle from Leibniz, but this didn't prevent him from castigating its originator for not understanding it properly. Schopenhauer points out that Leibniz had not clearly distinguished between various causes and effects, which Schopenhauer divided into his four types. Logical causes give a priori effects. That is, these are true *prior* to experience and are in no way dependent upon it. For example, the statement: "An octopus has eight legs." Physical causes, on the other hand, explain changes that take place in the physical world: for example, lightning, carbonized rabbit. Mathematical causes produce geometrical proofs. This is clear to us every time we rely upon $2 + 2 = 4$ to prove that mathematical space can have ten dimensions. And moral causes provide the motives for our actions. Action: son's unreasonable behavior at home. Motive: jealousy of mother's literary success, hypocritical disapproval of her lax moral behavior, insufficient admiration for aforesaid son's philosophic genius, etc.

Schopenhauer stresses that all these causes and effects belong to, and operate solely within, the phenomenal world. The noumenal world, the Kantian world of the thing-in-itself that supports this phenomenal world, which for Schopenhauer is replaced by the Will, does not take part in this chain of cause and effect. Causation can apply only in the world we experience. The Will does not act as a causative agent.

Schopenhauer supports this surprising claim with a powerful argument. He claims that we all have access to this world beyond the phenomenal world where the Will operates in its ghostly fashion. This happens when we seek to know ourselves. In the ordinary course of events we perceive ourselves just as we perceive the phenomena of the outer world. These are external perceptions. But we are also aware of ourselves "from within." On such occasions we are aware of ourselves as participating in the Will. On the one hand we can perceive ourselves operating in the physical world of cause and effect, but we also intuit and are aware of the Will within us. This we may glimpse as the Will to Life whose ghostly presence informs all our actions. Schopenhauer argues that this does not directly cause our actions, it somehow underlies them.

As a piece of rational philosophical argument this may not appear particularly convincing. It er, a deep and perceptive outline of human action—one that was way ahead of its time. As a tentative description of how the unconscious works, it immediately becomes much more convincing.

Although we can be aware of our actions on these two levels—act, Will—it is difficult to separate the two. Schopenhauer views the Will as a universal force that supports or irradiates all phenomena. As individuals we are merely a tiny part of this all-embracing blind Will. At this point Schopenhauer's argument faces an obvious objection. We may be aware of a will operating within us—yet most of us would probably describe this as individual willpower rather than participation in some universal force. This is how we apprehend it, or are aware of it. Even those who might see this will as part of a collective unconscious would find it difficult to enlarge this collective to include all that is embraced by Schopenhauer's transcendental, universe-permeating Will.

But philosophy is not a democratic process, any more than science is. Just because most of us

34

once believed that the earth was the center of the universe did not make it so. Likewise, just because most of us vaguely apprehend the will within us as individual—rather than the Will— does not defeat Schopenhauer's argument. Countless vague individual perceptions can sometimes be swept aside by just one vision of Copernican sweep and clarity.

To illustrate: just a year before Schopenhauer's death there appeared a scientific idea that would change the world forever. This was an idea that has arguably transformed our view of ourselves more than any idea before or since. In 1859 Charles Darwin published his *Origin of Species,* showing how all living species had evolved according to the "survival of the fittest." Much profound historical and contemporary thinking could not survive the emergence of this idea. Religion, philosophy, culture, even civilization—all felt the cold wind of an entirely new universe, one hitherto unimagined by humanity. The exalted species of *homo sapiens*—God's favorite, the purpose of all creation—was suddenly reduced to an accidental product of evolutionary development. Very little would survive this "hit and miss" idea intact. Science too was forced to embark upon a profound reexamination of its foundations. Even mathematics was not immune.

Perhaps the most poetically profound and satisfying philosophical conception of mathematics had been produced by the Arabs around the eighth century. In this view, to understand mathematics was to understand the mind of God. (Almost a thousand years later, Newton too believed this.) The absence of a God at work in the world of evolution implied that the same was true of mathematics. But if so, where did mathematics actually *exist*? Did it exist in the world or only in the minds of mathematicians? Was it *our* way of seeing the world, our imposition upon the undifferentiated flow of our experience? Or was $2 + 2 = 4$ true even when there were no minds to conceive of this? In what sense could mathematics be true when there was no such thing as numbers? Were mathematical truths somehow "out there" waiting to be discovered, or did we construct them from basic axioms and definitions for which we ourselves were wholly responsible? Philosophers of mathematics are still arguing over this.

In many ways the plight of mathematics epitomized the condition of all knowledge in the new evolutionary era. Nothing any more had a divine external guarantee. Nothing would be the same in this brave new scientific world. Such problems would devastate much pre-Darwinian thinking: Schopenhauer's was perhaps the only philosophy that was actually *deepened* by Darwin.

I may conceive of an individual willpower at work inside me, a will-to-survive that permeates my actions in a way of which I am often unaware. But when I view all living things in terms of Darwin's "survival of the fittest," it is possible to understand that my individual willpower may well be a minor manifestation of some universal Will. Here was no mere collective unconscious: Schopenhauer's Will drove through the entire universe. Several of Schopenhauer's disciples seized upon Darwin as a confirmation of his philosophy of Will.

However, this argument is based upon a misunderstanding of Darwinian thought (and, by implication, a misconception of Schopenhauer too). "Survival of the fittest" does not necessarily include willpower of any sort, even in the most variegated, sublimated, or degraded form. Darwin's famous slogan simply describes *what happens*—it does not describe any force that makes it happen. Indeed, his description of *how* evolution happens would seem to be the very opposite of will of any sort. Darwin saw *adaptation* as the means of survival. Blending in, adaptation to circumstance, giving way, bending to the wind—rather than assertion, domination, conspicuousness—have arguably proved the most effective evolutionary methods. If there is any underlying principle that describes how the universe "works," Schopenhauer's Will would certainly not seem to fit the bill. Except in one vital aspect: namely, the ultimate indifference to humanity with which the universe operates. And in this Schopenhauer *was* confirmed by Darwin. Schopenhauer saw this indifference as evil, because it destroyed human good, operating as it did without regard for human morality. This Will was certainly cold, unfeeling, inhuman, etc., but it was at bottom a morally neutral force. Good and evil (motive and action) belonged in the physical world, as Schopenhauer argued. His frequent stigmatization of the Will as evil essentially contradicted his own argument. Schopenhauer was aware of this inconsistency, and suggested that the Will was evil only in so far as it appeared as such to us.

As Schopenhauer emphasizes, the only way we can know the Will is through our inner apprehension of its role in our own lives. But if we can only know this Will by introspection, then strictly speaking we cannot be said to know its central supporting (or driving) role in the world of phenomena. We are aware of only one tiny aspect of the Will amidst an all-encompassing world of phenomena. This is essentially solipsism—the situation where I alone exist. Nothing else is real but my inner awareness of the Will and my experience of phenomena.

All philosophies have faced the difficulty of solipsism—a cul-de-sac out of which it is all but impossible to argue. In the most rigid sense, there is no escape from this lonely situation. Schopen-hauer's philosophy also falls foul of such stric-tures, but his argument has its persuasive force nonetheless. I may not be able to prove that oth-ers have their own independent existence (and el-ement of Will), or that they experience the world much as I do, but I can *infer* it. My experience, and the consistency of what appear to be their reactions to me, lead me to believe that I am en-countering other beings like myself.

With mental persistence we can reduce our-selves to a state of solipsism, the scrupulously limited condition of the Beckett hero. This can prove both revealing and philosophically fruit-ful. How little we know for certain of the world and our life in it. But the habits of common sense soon return us to the so-called sane world of our fellow human beings.

So far so good. But Schopenhauer extends this inference from our introspection of will to the all-pervasive Will. As we have seen, notions such as the unconscious mind and evolution lend some weight to this argument. But such notions were not available to Schopenhauer when he created his philosophy; as a result, his limited, strictly philosophical argument is less convincing. Here, it appears, the exceptional prescience of his understanding outstripped his ability to explain what he felt to be true. Intuition preceded analysis. The reader is convinced on the poetic rather than the philosophical level. And this was certainly true of those contemporaries who embraced Schopenhauer's philosophy during the last years of his fame. Schopenhauer had discovered a poetic truth that found considerable psychological rapport—but as an intellectually arguable truth it remained ahead of its time.

Be this as it may, Schopenhauer proceeds to base his entire philosophy upon this central notion of the Will, which permeates all things. It is seen as evil, or indifferent to humanity, and as such is the origin of suffering in the world. The world is thus essentially evil, or indifferent to us: a place of irredeemable misery, illuminated with occasional flashes of horror. Here Schopenhauer's misanthropic streak comes into its own. Not for nothing would he become known one day as "the philosopher of pessimism." His vision of the world was one of sophisticated, remote (and often highly witty) distaste. For long passages he revels in the stupidity of human behavior, uncovering with acute psychological acumen the hypocrisy and self-centeredness that lie at the root of so much human activity. All such things (and such things were *all*) were manifestations of the Will. This was what drove the world.

The only way to escape from this deluge of wickedness was to lessen its force within oneself, to overcome this Will that drives the appetites and desires, the lusts of the flesh and ambition. Self-abnegation and withdrawal from life were the only answer. The sole effective attitude to life, and the multifarious manifestations of the Will, was withdrawal into a stoic asceticism. Here the influence of oriental religion on Schopenhauer's philosophy is plain to see. The "religionless religion" of Buddhism carries much the same message. Similar thinking permeates the wisdom of the Hindu sages. But there is a subtle difference between Schopenhauer's advice and the goal of such oriental religion.

The ascetic withdrawal that he urges is all but identical (though his encouragement to will-less contemplation of works of art is not precisely the same as meditating on a lotus blossom). But it is the way Schopenhauer urges this denial of Will that differentiates it from the wisdom of the East. Schopenhauer's tone of voice is always unmistakably his own. He never loses his style. His writing remains worldly, sophisticated, and witty at all times. What is missing is the spirituality of the East. Schopenhauer's stoicism harks back to the stoicism that developed among the intellectual upper class of the late Roman Empire, during its more disgraceful periods of bloodletting, sensual viciousness, and imperial degeneracy. Schopenhauer's is the world-weariness and disgust of the toga rather than the loincloth. He may appear to advocate much the same behavior, but following this course will bring about no redeeming spiritual enlightenment. The will-less contemplation of a work of art may give us a momentary aesthetic experience, but this is hardly a vision of nirvana. We must withdraw from the hideous manifestation of the Will for the sake of self-preservation (which is at the same time a form of self-destruction). Our only reward is the meager understanding that the Will is utterly evil and functions as a nasty joke at our expense. The end product Schopenhauer often seems to have in mind is an austere gentleman who frequents the art galleries, rather than a skeletal mystic.

And indeed, this frugal, gentlemanly figure is very much how Schopenhauer saw himself. Alas, the facts paint a rather different picture. Throughout his life Schopenhauer lived in bourgeois comfort, denying himself few of the normal accoutrements of such a well-heeled leisurely existence. His suits were hand-tailored from the finest materials, he ate in restaurants, and he enjoyed the company of good-looking young women. Not for one moment did he contemplate giving up his private income for any saintly existence without a housekeeper; he continued to have love affairs of a most unexalted nature; and he enjoyed eating large meals. (As he once replied to an inquisitive dining companion: "Sir, true I eat three times as much as you, but I have

44

three times as much brains as you.") Yet he did find time to submit himself to regular bouts of will-less aesthetic appreciation. He was keen on literature, going to concerts and art galleries, and often visited the theatre (and not just to pick up chorus girls).

Schopenhauer had very definite ideas on art and wrote a great deal on the subject. In his view, the highest form of art was music, which descended through poetry to its lowest form in architecture. (Light romantic novels, such as those of Johanna Schopenhauer, do not appear on this artistic scale.)

When Schopenhauer finished *The World as Will and Representation,* he sent the manuscript to a publisher with a characteristically bashful covering note: "This book in times to come will be the source and occasion of a hundred other books." As it happens, this turned out to be an extremely modest underestimation. But not to begin with. For many years, decades even, Schopenhauer's work was spectacularly unsuccessful. Sixteen years later the publishers finally informed Schopenhauer that almost all of the small first edition of his masterpiece had been pulped as waste paper. Schopenhauer's reaction to this lack of acclaim from his contemporaries was typical: "Would a musician be flattered by the loud applause of an audience if he knew that they were nearly all deaf?") But this humiliation and acerbic forbearance all lay in the future.

Confident of fame now that he had delivered his masterpiece to the publishers, Schopenhauer embarked on a long holiday in Italy. Before setting out he had written to Goethe, who had sent him a letter of introduction to Byron. The maverick British poet was living in Venice at the time, which happened to be on Schopenhauer's itinerary. While Schopenhauer was walking along the Lido with a woman he had picked up, Byron happened to gallop past on his horse. The woman shrieked and passed into a rapture at the sight of the great romantic hero. Schopenhauer, stricken with jealousy, decided against using his letter of introduction from Goethe. (In years to come Schopenhauer was to cite this as an instance of "women preventing mankind from greatness.") Schopenhauer continued wandering through Italy for a year—irritating the international artists' colony in the Caffe Greco in Rome with his provocative opinions (advocating polytheism, referring to the apostles as "twelve philistines from Jerusalem," etc.), and writing home that in Italy he "enjoyed not only her beauty but also her beauties."

In 1819 *The World as Will and Representation* was published. This not only contained Schopenhauer's entire system in almost finished form but was to be the pinnacle of his thought—which was not to develop further in any significant way during the ensuing forty years of his life. By 1820 Schopenhauer was beginning to become distinctly impatient at his lack of world fame. He decided to take matters into his own hands and secured a post as *privatdozent* at the University of Berlin, where Hegel was teaching. Hegel had now settled like a thick blanket of snow over the green fields and woodlands of German philosophy. Nothing of the real landscape was visible beneath this muffling, colorless shroud of obscurity—and philosophers had been reduced to creating quaint snowmen, lobbing dialectical snowballs at one another, and skating skillfully across the frozen ponds of abstraction. The world flocked to hear Santa Claus deliver his lectures.

Schopenhauer spotted at once that his rival to the philosophic heavyweight title of Germany was a phony, and announced that he would deliver his lectures at precisely the same time as Hegel's. Schopenhauer was flabbergasted when no one turned up. To console himself after delivering his solipsistic lectures, he took up with a nineteen-year-old actress called Caroline Medon. This was just the kind of delightful young person he was looking for, he decided, and began contemplating marriage (though without informing Caroline). He was outraged when he discovered that she had several other lovers, and he offered her money to give them up. Then he decided that he needed another yearlong holiday in Italy to think things over. Caroline doesn't seem to have been invited, but when Schopenhauer left her behind in Berlin he promised that he would be with her in spirit. Caroline gave a little more substance to this aery promise when she wrote to him a few weeks later, announcing that she was pregnant. Schopenhauer gallantly decided to remain with her in spirit, and continued his long tour of Italy. By the time he returned to Berlin, Caroline had given birth to a son.

It was around this time that Schopenhauer became involved in another incident that was to have unforeseen long-term consequences. One afternoon he was waiting in his apartment, keenly anticipating a tryst with Caroline. One can only assume that he was listening intently at the front door for her approach, because he happened to hear Frau Marquet, the forty-five-year-old seamstress from next door, gossiping with a couple of her friends on the landing. Irritated by the continuing gossip (and probably wishing to avoid becoming a target of it himself), Schopenhauer opened his door and abruptly told his neighbor to do her gossiping elsewhere. Frau Marquet took umbrage at being interrupted by this rude little man, and refused to budge. Whereupon Schopenhauer became extremely irritated. He ended up grabbing her around the waist and removing her bodily while she kicked and screamed.

Frau Marquet took Schopenhauer to court on a charge of assault, and Schopenhauer was given a small fine of twenty thaler. But by now Frau Marquet had discovered that Schopenhauer was a rich man, and she lodged an appeal, alleging that as a result of the fall she had suffered when Schopenhauer threw her out, she was now completely paralyzed on her right side and could barely move her arm. Schopenhauer contested this vigorously, and the case dragged on in the usual fashion so that the lawyers could earn their fees. Eventually, six years later, Schopenhauer lost the case. His superior sarcastic attitude had not endeared him to the court, and he was ordered to pay Frau Marquet fifteen thalers a quarter for as long as her injury persisted. Frau Marquet evidently took this judgment as a challenge and managed to prolong the effects of her alleged injury for the next twenty years, until her death. When Schopenhauer learned of her demise and realized that he would no longer have to pay, he wittily recorded in Latin in his journal: "Obit anus, abit onus" (which isn't as rude as it sounds, and merely means: "The old woman dies, the burden departs").

Meanwhile, copies of *The World as Will and Representation* continued to gather dust in the bookshops. Still Schopenhauer was being deprived of the fame that was his due. And to add insult to injury, Hegel was still packing them in at his lectures (while a nearby lecture hall remained conspicuously empty). Having tried the direct approach to sabotaging his great rival, Schopenhauer now decided to try a more conventional philosophical tactic. He wrote describing Hegelianism as "the impudence of a scribbler of nonsense," characterizing its originator as "a flat-headed illiterate charlatan." But still no one took notice.

In the meantime Schopenhauer decided to try his hand at translation, making plans to translate Hume into German and Kant into English. Unfortunately nothing came of these schemes, which would certainly have been of incalculable benefit to philosophic circles on both sides of the

North Sea. Nothing came of his plans for marriage, either. He appears to have loved Caroline
Medon but wasn't sure whether her social stand-
ing or her illegitimate child would be fitting for
the world-famous philosopher he would surely
become. Then he (wrongly) suspected that she
had tuberculosis, which was regarded socially in
much the same compassionate light as AIDS
nowadays. A good psychiatrist would probably
have sorted Schopenhauer out, but it was still
thirty years before Freud arrived on the scene
and could later become deeply influenced by
Schopenhauer's philosophy, sufficient for him to
discover the very method by which he might
have cured its author. Much as this knot defies
unraveling, so Schopenhauer continued to dither
between his loving ego and his forbidding paternal superego. The affair with Caroline dragged
on and off for years, and long after it was finally
over he was to remember her in his will. Though
at the same time he characteristically excluded
all claims by a certain young Carl Ludwig
Medon. The man who claimed to understand the
world, and everything that was wrong with it,

52

never did understand what was wrong with himself.

In 1831 cholera swept through Berlin and Schopenhauer fled. (This was the outbreak that killed his arch-rival Hegel.) Two years later, at the age of forty-five, Schopenhauer settled in Frankfurt. He was to remain in this city for the next twenty-eight years, living a bachelor life whose extreme regularity was modeled on that of his hero, Kant. This is the image of Schopenhauer that has passed on to posterity—the figure we love to loathe: the acid old fart of Frankfurt (to rise to the Schopenhauerian level of philosophic character assessment). He took to dressing in old-fashioned clothes (though impeccably tailored) and developed an obsession about noise. ("I have long been of the opinion that the quantity of noise anyone can comfortably endure is in inverse proportion to his mental powers.")

After rising late and taking his coffee, he would read for three hours. Then he would play his flute (Rossini, "*con amore*"). After this it was time for a late luncheon at the round table in the prestigious Englischer Hof on Rossmarkt. In the

53

afternoon he would retire to the reading rooms of the Casino Society to read the latest copy of *The Times* which had arrived from London, then he would set off for a long walk—a familiar local figure, striding briskly down the pavement talking to himself. On these walks he would invariably be accompanied by his poodle, which he called *Atma*: Indian for "the world's soul." As befitted its exalted title, the poodle would trot silently and inscrutably at his muttering master's side, enacting this instructive tableau of the philosopher and his riddle. On his return home he would read long into the night while the world and its soul slept (the latter at his feet).

Schopenhauer read widely, in literature and philosophy; and after nineteen years of "silent indignation" at his lack of fame he published a second philosophical work, *On the Will in Nature.* The preface of this work contains a hilarious invective against Hegel which has little to do with philosophy, and the book itself is mainly an elaboration of points in his earlier great work. He also brought out another edition of *The World as Will and Representation,* but this too

54

did not succeed in breaking down "the resistance of a dull world."

In this second edition Schopenhauer expands upon ideas that he now considered to be insufficiently developed in the first edition. Here we find the full version of his ideas on political philosophy and the role of the state. These are heavily influenced by his pessimistic view of human nature. In his political philosophy Schopenhauer followed on from the seventeenth-century English political philosopher Thomas Hobbes, author of *The Leviathan*. According to Hobbes, without government "the life of man [is] solitary, poor, nasty, brutish, and short." These were sentiments with which Schopenhauer heartily concurred. (Indeed, there are times when he appeared to find this the case even when people *did* have government.) Hobbes saw the origin of the state in the natural wish of people to overcome this primitive state of affairs. Thus any form of government was better than none. From this Hobbes made a giant leap to the conclusion that people should therefore conform to the dictates of whatever government they found themselves under. Life in any state, be it ever so malign, was always better than a life that was "nasty, brutish, and short"—where nothing constructive of any sort could be achieved.

Schopenhauer concurs with this view, though injecting his own characteristic element of wit and misanthropy. For him, humanity essentially consists of nothing but "beasts of prey." The state acts as a "muzzle" to these wild animals, transforming them into "harmless grass-consuming cattle." Humanity does not choose between Good and Evil—instead, as we have seen, it is driven by an evil universal Will. Such beings can have no real idea of justice; all they know is a basic negative version of this ideal. When they suffer an infringement of their will, they experience pain and indignation—which they see as injustice. Yet at the same time these base creatures are always seeking for opportunities to inflict themselves on others—impeding *their* will and arousing *their* sense of injustice. Thus the fundamental purpose of the state must be to prevent this from happening. The citizen must at all costs be deterred from inflicting his will upon others in a detrimental fashion.

Enlightened thinkers, from Kant to the romantics, had previously developed a more benevolent view of the state. Its purpose was to improve the morals of its citizens, benignly encouraging them to become better human beings. The state should be a force for the good, giving meaning to the lives of its citizens, instead of being simply a "necessary evil," checking their baser instincts. Schopenhauer perceptively saw what the result of this seemingly more benevolent state could be. Such "encouragement" to become better citizens led to the imposition of a collective will, or to the cultivation of a uniform behavior that the state considered to be improving. It left no room for individuality, for the citizen to develop in his own fashion.

Although the romantic and enlightened view of the state may seem more immediately appealing than Schopenhauer's grim pessimism, in practice such "improvement" of the citizens by the state could lead to the worst excesses. Schopenhauer abhorred both the revolutionaries of the left and the authoritarian right-wing Prussian state (so beloved of Hegel). Both sought to impose their own version of how to improve the lot of the people—one by progressive egalitarianism, the other by conservative authoritarianism. The state's conception of values would either be created or preserved—but either way it would be imposed at the expense of any alternative set of values. Schopenhauer was to be proved correct in his assessment of the similar outcome of these apparent opposites. The worst excesses of state "improvement" in the following twentieth century would be communist and fascist.

Despite his well-heeled and protected way of life, Schopenhauer found that he was not immune from the vagaries of politics. He was to receive a nasty fright when uprisings broke out all over Europe in 1848, the "year of revolution." The disturbances in Germany not only upset his daily routine, they also threatened to disrupt the commercial sources of his private income. What was the world coming to? Fortunately the unrest in Frankfurt was quickly put down, and it was soon safe for a gentleman of independent means to walk the streets with his poodle. The revolting citizens had demonstrated all too plainly that his assessment of their character was correct. Such creatures needed to be muzzled, not encouraged—to shout abuse at a law-abiding philosopher accompanied by the world's soul. But other indignities were less easy to live with. The deep inner pain at his lack of success continued to rancor, though he did his best to disguise this. The long wait for recognition had now persisted for decades, and despite his acerbic buoyancy in public he was slowly becoming reconciled to the fact that his life had been nothing but one long failure.

At the age of sixty-three Schopenhauer decided to publish his essays and maxims, but no one was interested in printing them. In the end he managed to persuade a minor Berlin bookseller to bring out a small edition, by promising to finance it himself. This work he called *Parerga and Paralipomena* (from the Latin "Ornaments and Omissions"). It contains a series of bitterly witty pieces on a wide range of topics. These essays and aphorisms remain as fresh, perceptive, and provocative today as they were when first published. Schopenhauer's position is often aggressively conservative, laced with an incongruous anarchistic streak, and leavened with witty egoism. His views on women are predictably unacceptable. For example: "Only a male intellect clouded by sexual desire could call the stunted, narrow-shouldered, broad-hipped, and short-legged sex the fair sex." (Viewed as a mirror of its author, this scarcely reflects favorably on the state of his intellect or the female company he kept.) But he has interesting unconservative things to say about monogamy, suicide, the church's involvement in the slave trade, ethics, thinking for oneself, and ghosts. *Parerga and Paralipomena* is by far the most readable work written by any major philosopher since Plato, and remains surprisingly in tune with modern sensibilities despite certain easily recognizable grotesqueries. Yet, though this work certainly reflects Schopenhauer's philosophical position, it can hardly be called philosophy. It remains for the most part a philosophical eccentricity: not quite in the same comic category as Leibniz's scheme for flooding the state of Hanover, Berkeley's proposals for tar water, or Wittgenstein's reflections on culture—but at the same time not entirely free of unintended farce.

In April 1853 *Parerga and Paralipomena* was given a favorable notice in the *Westminster Review* of London, which was edited by George Eliot (who obviously didn't pay much attention to the books she sent out for review). In those days German intellectuals had a healthy if somewhat misplaced respect for British thought. At once all the German intellectual periodicals took notice of Schopenhauer's work, and he became famous overnight. The last person to rejoice at this fairy tale ending to his endeavors was Schopenhauer himself, who stuck resolutely to his routine and remained as crotchety as ever (though in fact he secretly exulted in his success, covertly asking his few remaining acquaintances to seek out all mentions of him in the papers so that he could read them over breakfast). Young aficionados of the new philosophic star flocked to the Englischer Hof and bribed the waiters for seats at the round table, where their enthusiasm was subjected to the customary biting wit. These aficionados went away smarting but overjoyed—convinced they had been insulted by the finest mind in Europe.

At the age of sixty-five, after more than thirty-five years of waiting, "the Nile had reached Cairo," as Schopenhauer put it. He loved the fame that he genuinely deserved—but died within seven years, on September 21, 1860.

Schopenhauer's combative pessimistic writings were to prove a deep influence on such disparate figures as Wagner, Freud, Tolstoy, Nietzsche, and Jacob Burckhardt, to name but a few. Most of these men read only his essays, but they certainly gleaned the chilling message of his metaphysics. Yet how could Schopenhauer really claim to know that behind the world of appearances lay a cold, dark, unrelenting and unthinking Will? According to Schopenhauer, we are all given the opportunity to see behind the world of appearances—by looking inside ourselves.

Afterword

Schopenhauer didn't attract followers, he attracted disciples. Such was the impact of his utterly novel approach to philosophy on the staid intellectual world of mid-nineteenth-century Germany. Yet not all these disciples were easily led sycophants. Among them were some of the finest minds of the next generation.

Long before the belated arrival of Schopenhauer's fame, his work had been discovered by the young Richard Wagner. Its disruptive effect overwhelmed him, and in the 1848 revolution Wagner (in the company of the anarchist Mikhail Bakunin) was inspired to take to the barricades in Leipzig. As we have seen, Schopenhauer was horrified by such behavior, which could easily have cut off his private income (and thus forced the philosopher to embark upon the asceticism he so recommended). Wagner had been intoxicated with Schopenhauer's writing and filled with Schopenhauerian pessimism. In his youthful enthusiasm Wagner blended this seemingly incompatible combination into an anarchic nihilism that was all his own. For years afterward he continued to gain artistic inspiration from reading Schopenhauer, despite the fact that his understanding of the philosopher's work bore little semblance to what Schopenhauer had intended. (Siegfried is not noted for his oriental resignation.)

Schopenhauer's appeal to the creative temperament has continued to the present day, inspiring almost as many different responses as it has creators. Figures as disparate as Thomas Mann, James Joyce, Samuel Beckett, and Thomas Bernhard all found a rapport in Schopenhauer and his pessimistic outlook.

But Schopenhauer's effect on ensuing philosophers was to be even more drastic, and even more disparate. The hapless Philipp Mainländer took Schopenhauer's pessimistic view of the world to its extreme with regard to the problems of both society and the individual. The only way to solve the problem of the poor was to give them everything they desired: this would immediately convince them of the vanity of such things and the futility of life. They would then be able to face up to the problem of individual existence, which Mainländer solved by committing suicide.

Nietzsche decided to take a different approach. By far the most brilliant and profound thinker to be affected by Schopenhauer, Nietzsche simply turned Schopenhauer's idea of the Will on its head. Instead of the world being driven by a blind evil Will, which could be combated only by ascetic withdrawal, Nietzsche advocated the Will to Power. Here lay the driving force within all human nature, and the great men of history had been its finest manifestation.

Adopting a cunning blend of both Schopenhauer's and Nietzsche's notions of the Will, Freud was later to propose the notion of the subconscious mind. More recently, Schopenhauer had a profound effect on the very last of the traditional philosophers. Freud's fellow Viennese Ludwig Wittgenstein was profoundly influenced by both Schopenhauer's pessimism and his inherently mystical view of the world. Wittgenstein's famous dictum, "About that which we cannot speak, we must remain silent" (*Tractatus Logico-Philosophicus* 7.00) may be speaking ostensibly of language and meaning, but it bears an uncanny resemblance to Schopenhauer's advocacy of withdrawal from the dark unseen Will that remains forever beyond our understanding.

From Schopenhauer's Writings

When we perceive and consider the existence, life, and activity of any natural creature, e.g., an animal, it appears to us to be essentially an inscrutable mystery, despite all we can learn about it from zoology and comparative anatomy. But why does nature forever refuse to answer such questions? Surely, like everything great, she is open, communicative, and even naive. So why does nature forever refuse to answer such questioning? The reason we have no answer can only be because our question was incorrectly formulated, arose from our own narrow-minded assumptions, or was self-contradictory. Is it possible that there is a chain of grounds and consequents which must remain forever unfathomable to us? Certainly not. Just the opposite, such matters are unfathomable because we search for grounds and consequents in a sphere which is foreign to such things.

—Parerga and Paralipomena, Sec 65

Thing-in-itself signifies that which exists independently of our perception by means of the senses. In other words, it is that which really and truly is. Democritus called this matter; in the end so did Locke; for Kant it was an *x*; and for me it is *Will*.

—Parerga and Paralipomena, Sec 61

Only at one point do I have access to the world other than as representation. This is in myself. When I perceive my body, this is representation. . . . But I am also aware of those urges which give rise to this representation: this is the Will. Only within myself do I have this dual knowledge of Will and representation.

—The World as Will and Representation

The dual knowledge we each have of the nature and activity of our own body, which is given to us in two completely different ways, is now clear. We will therefore make further use of this as a key to the essential character of every phenomenon in nature. All objects which are not our own body, and thus not given to our knowledge in a double way (but only as representation), we shall judge to be similar to our own body. And as we know they are similar to our body in the first way, we shall assume that they are similar in the second way. Thus, when we take away their existence as representation, all that remains is what we call *Will*—just the same as in our own bodies. What other kind of existence or reality should we attribute to the rest of the material world? How else can we conceive of such a world? For besides Will and representation nothing else is known to us, or even conceivable.

—*The World as Will and Representation*,
2nd Book

We complain that we live in ignorance, unable to understand the connection between all existence, and in particular the connection between our particular existence and the whole of existence. Our life is not only short, but our knowledge of it severely limited. We can't look back beyond our birth, or forward beyond our death. Our consciousness is a momentary flicker in the midst of night. It appears as if some malevolent demon has limited our ability to know, so that he can enjoy our discomfort.

But such a complaint is unjustified. It is based on the mistaken idea that the world was created by an *intellect,* and as a result originated as a *mental picture* (or representation) before it became real. According to this mistaken view, the world originated from knowledge, and was thus accessible to knowledge—capable of being analyzed and completely understood by it. But the truth is, what we complain of not knowing is not known by any one or any thing, and is in itself absolutely unknowable. It is in fact inconceivable.

—*Parerga and Paralipomena,* Sec 67

70

The state to which death restores us is our original state. That is to say, the one peculiar to our true nature, whose essential force manifests itself by producing and maintaining the life that we lose in death. This is the state of the thing-in-itself as distinct from the phenomenon. In this original state cerebral knowledge, which deals only with phenomena, is thus superfluous. So it disappears. Its disappearance is for us identical with the disappearance of the phenomenal world, which was its medium, and whose disappearance leaves it redundant. Even if, while we were in this original state, we were offered this animal consciousness, we would refuse it—just as a cured cripple refuses crutches. Thus whoever begrudges the impending loss of his cerebral consciousness—which is merely a phenomena and can only be used in the phenomenal realm—is like the converted Greenlanders who refused the idea of heaven because there were no seals in it.

—*Parerga and Paralipomena*, Sec 139

All this means is that life can be regarded as a dream and death as the awakening from it. In which case the individual personality belongs to the dreaming rather than the waking state. Subsequently, death appears to the individual personality as annihilation. On the other hand, if we look upon life as a dream, death no longer becomes a transition to something strange or new, but merely a return to our original state, where life is seen merely as a brief episode.

—*Parerga and Paralipomena,* Sec 139

Still more preposterous is the theory that the state is the condition of moral freedom, and in this way the condition of morality. Freedom lies beyond phenomena, and indeed beyond human arrangements. As we have seen, the state is hardly directed against egoism in general. On the contrary, it arose through egoism and exists only to further it. This egoism is well aware of where its best interests lie. It proceeds methodically, forsaking the narrowly individual point of view in favor of the universal point of view, thus becoming the common egoism of all. The state is there-fore created on the understanding that its citizens will not behave morally—that is, choose to act in the right way for moral reasons (i.e., for the good of all). For if this were the case there would be no need for the state in the first place. So the state, which is intended to bring about the well-being of its citizens, is by no means directed against egoism in general. It is only directed against the multiplicity of particular egoisms and their deleterious effect on the collective egoism which desires the general well-being.

—*The World as Will and Representation,*
4th Book

Money is human happiness in theory; anyone who is no longer capable of actual happiness longs for money.

When will replaces knowledge, the result is *obstinacy.*

If you want to know your true feelings toward

someone, note the immediate impression made on you by the arrival of an unexpected letter from him (or her).

—*Parerga and Paralipomena,*
Sec 320, 321, 326

Chronology of Significant Philosophical Dates

6th C B.C.   The beginning of Western philosophy with Thales of Miletus.

End of
6th C B.C.   Death of Pythagoras.

399 B.C.   Socrates sentenced to death in Athens.

c 387 B.C.   Plato founds the Academy in Athens, the first university.

335 B.C.   Aristotle founds the Lyceum in Athens, a rival school to the Academy.

324 A.D.	Emperor Constantine moves capital of Roman Empire to Byzantium.
400 A.D.	St. Augustine writes his *Confessions*. Philosophy absorbed into Christian theology.
410 A.D.	Sack of Rome by Visigoths heralds opening of Dark Ages.
529 A.D.	Closure of Academy in Athens by Emperor Justinian marks end of Hellenic thought.
Mid-13th C	Thomas Aquinas writes his commentaries on Aristotle. Era of Scholasticism.
1453	Fall of Byzantium to Turks, end of Byzantine Empire.
1492	Columbus reaches America. Renaissance in Florence and revival of interest in Greek learning.
1543	Copernicus publishes *On the Revolution of the Celestial Orbs*, proving mathematically that the earth revolves around the sun.

1633	Galileo forced by church to recant heliocentric theory of the universe.
1641	Descartes publishes his *Meditations*, the start of modern philosophy.
1677	Death of Spinoza allows publication of his *Ethics*.
1687	Newton publishes *Principia*, introducing concept of gravity.
1689	Locke publishes *Essay Concerning Human Understanding*. Start of empiricism.
1710	Berkeley publishes *Principles of Human Knowledge*, advancing empiricism to new extremes.
1716	Death of Leibniz.
1739–1740	Hume publishes *Treatise of Human Nature*, taking empiricism to its logical limits.
1781	Kant, awakened from his "dogmatic slumbers" by Hume, publishes *Critique of Pure Reason*.

Great era of German metaphysics begins.

1807   Hegel publishes *The Phenomenology of Mind*, high point of German metaphysics.

1818   Schopenhauer publishes *The World as Will and Representation*, introducing Indian philosophy into German metaphysics.

1889   Nietzsche, having declared "God is dead," succumbs to madness in Turin.

1921   Wittgenstein publishes *Tractatus Logico-Philosophicus*, claiming the "final solution" to the problems of philosophy.

1920s   Vienna Circle propounds Logical Positivism.

1927   Heidegger publishes *Being and Time*, heralding split between analytical and Continental philosophy.

1943   Sartre publishes *Being and Nothingness*, advancing

Heidegger's thought and instigating existentialism.

1953   Posthumous publication of Wittgenstein's *Philosophical Investigations*. High era of linguistic analysis.

Chronology of Schopenhauer's Life

1788	Arthur Schopenhauer born in Danzig.
1793	Schopenhauer family leaves for Hamburg before Prussian occupation of Danzig.
1803–1804	Accompanies family on tour of Europe.
1805	Suicide of father.
1807	Moves to Weimar.
1811–1813	Studies in Berlin.

1814	Acrimonious end to relationship with mother.
1819	First edition of *The World as Will and Representation* published.
1820	Lectures in Berlin a dismal failure.
1821	Throws Frau Marquet down stairs and loses court case, incurring regular payments.
1833	Settles in Frankfurt.
1844	Second edition of *The World as Will and Representation*.
1851	Publishes *Parerga and Paralipomena*.
1853	Achieves fame at last.
1860	Dies in Frankfurt.

82

Recommended Reading

Patrick Gardiner, *Schopenhauer* (Thoemmes Press, 1997). A penetrating analysis of Schopenhauer's thought, covering all his major ideas.

Friedrich Nietzsche, *Untimely Meditations*, translated by R. J. Hollingdale (Cambridge University Press, 1984). Contains the classic essay "Schopenhauer as Educator" by his most famous disciple.

Rudiger Safranski, *Schopenhauer and the Wild Years of Philosophy* (Harvard University Press, 1991). The classic work on Schopenhauer's life and philosophy—as easy to read as the master himself, and filled with incident and insight.

Arthur Schopenhauer, *Essays and Aphorisms*, translated and selected by R. J. Hollingdale (Penguin,

1973). A highly readable and equally controversial selection from *Parerga and Paralipomena*.

Arthur Schopenhauer, *The World as Will and Representation*, translated by E. F. Payne, 2 vols. (Dover, 1966). Schopenhauer's masterwork, which was ignored for so long. Exciting philosophy and filled with erudition.

Index

A NOTE ON THE AUTHOR

Paul Strathern has lectured in philosophy and mathematics and now lives and writes in London. A Somerset Maugham prize winner, he is also the author of books on history and travel as well as five novels. His articles have appeared in a great many publications, including the *Observer* (London) and the *Irish Times*. His own degree in philosophy was earned at Trinity College, Dublin.